A SHUTTLE IN THE CRYPT

By the same author

Plays

A Dance in the Forest
The Lion and the Jewel
The Swamp Dwellers
The Trials of Brother Jero
Jero's Metamorphosis
The Strong Breed
The Road
Kongi's Harvest
Camwood on the Leaves
Madmen and Specialists
Death and the King's Horseman
A Play of Giants
Opera Wonyosi
Requiem for a Futurologist

Novels

The Interpreters
Season of Anomy

Poetry

Idanre and Other Poems
Poems from Prison
Ogun Abibiman

Autobiography and Memoirs

Aké The Years of Childhood
The Man Died

A SHUTTLE
IN THE
CRYPT
WOLE
SOYINKA

REX COLLINGS/METHUEN

First published jointly in 1972 by
Rex Collings Ltd
6 Paddington Street W1
and Eyre Methuen & Co Ltd
11 New Fetter Lane EC4P 4EE

Reprinted jointly in 1986 by
Methuen London Ltd
11 New Fetter Lane EC4P 4EE
and Rex Collings Ltd
6 Paddington Street W1

Copyright © Wole Soyinka 1972

ISBN 0–413–28890–0

Printed in Great Britain
by Redwood Burn Ltd, Trowbridge, Wiltshire

CONTENTS

PREFACE

The shuttle is a unique species of the caged animal, a restless bolt of energy, a trapped weaver-bird yet charged in repose with unspoken forms and designs. In motion or at rest it is a secretive seed, shrine, kernel, phallus and well of creative mysteries. Self-identification with this essence of innate repletion was a natural weapon to employ against the dangers of an in-human isolation. It was never a mere poetic conceit; all events, thoughts, dreams, incidental phenomena were, in sheer self-protection perceived and absorbed into the loom-shuttle unity of such an existence.

Except for two or three poems in the section 'Poems of bread and earth' this volume consists of poems written in gaol in spite of the deprivation of reading and writing material in nearly two years of solitary confinement. It is a map of the course trodden by the mind, not a record of the actual struggle against a vegetable existence – that belongs in another place.

Chimes of Silence is central to the entire experience. The passage of five men to and through that travesty of looms, the gallows, was at once harrowing and consoling. Seeing nothing but sealed in a vault which drew in the sounds of it all, it was a private ritual solely for, solely witnessed by me. I listened to an enactment of death in the home of death, to the pulse of a shuttle slowing to its final moment of rest, towards that complete in-gathering of being which a shuttle in repose so palpably is. It was, in this sense, both horror and consolation.

The landscape of the poems is not uncommon; physical details differ, but finally the landscape of the loss of human contact is the same. 'Bearings' which is a topographical preface to the body of *Chimes* etches some of these physical details. Under *Phases of Peril*, 'Conversation at Night' seems at first a strange inclusion, but it was indeed this kind of evocation of events, yielding nothing but past and future evidence of the unchanging nature of humanity which set in process the worst moments of pessimism.

And it was this ever-recurrent awareness, this level of the loss of human contact that proved more corrosive than that purely physical loss upon which the little mind-butchers had based their hope.

WOLE SOYINKA
JULY, 1971

Phases of Peril

O ROOTS!

Roots, be an anchor at my keel
Shore my limbs against the wayward gale

Reach in earth for deep sustaining draughts
Potencies against my endless thirsts

Your surface runnels end in blinds, your courses
Choke on silt, stagnate in human curses

Feet of pilgrims pause by charted pools
Balm seeking. Dipped, their thirsty bowls

Raise bubbles of corruption, sludge
Of evil, graves unlaid to tears or dirge

Roots, I pray you lead away from streams
Of tainted seepage lest I, of these crimes

Partake, from fouled communion earth
In ashes scattered from a common hearth

Roots! lead away from treachery of the dark
From pit of acceptance, from the baited stake

Lend not image to a serpent spawn
Of lures, to monster prodigies of spleen

[1]

Do not, pride of sinews tunnel far
In secrets, yet surface close to guilty fear

To grasp of greed, to bane of spittle squalls
On quivers of green-awakening quills.

O Roots, be an anchor at my keel
Cord my thoughts from tensed, rock-suturing reel

Reach in earth to new sustaining draughts
Pierce her timeless hoards with keen-eyed shafts

Flush hours of staleness out to death's
Eternal sump. Arouse the captive breaths

Of springs and vaulted lakes, their waters draw
To seedling hands, to goals on threshing-floor

Roots, be the network of my large
Design, hold to your secret charge

All bedrock architecture raised to heal
Desert cries, desert lacerations; seal

In barks of age, test on battering-rams
Of your granite caps O breaker of dams

Pestle in earth mortar, ringer of chimes
In rock funnels, render mine Time's

Chaplets, and stress to your eternal season
These inward plinths I raise against unreason

Against the dark-sprung moment of the trap
Against the noontide thunderclap!

Pathfinder to the underworld, lead
My feet to core, to kernel seed

Draw me still to crucibles of earth's
Alchemistry, to rock and metal births

To vibrations of your tuning-fork.
Press these palms, that they shall join in talk,

In memories, sights, to blindfold passing ones
Borne to the eternal banquet on wine-tidal runs

Let my hands intertwine with theirs
Clear sap and dark, red flesh and ghost hairs

Cell chains as leaf and limb, vein
Of limb and rock, eyes in womb of grain

To a filter of impulses weave their bones
That combs of my marrow may, in kernel stones

Receive the roots of lightning from the sky
Storing light of their departed eye

[3]

Draw to earth all lethal pulses, that my cup
Of hands may echo fiery harmonies, and sup

At wedding-feasts of sky and earth. Thread
My hands to spring-rites, to green hands of the dead.

O Roots Roots. If it Shall Not Withstand!
If it shall cave to wind and choke in sands

Of wilderness, if it shall cinder in flash
Of the dearth-awaited, your coils unleash

Upon the last defence of sluices! The prow
Is pointed to a pull of undertows

A grey plunge in pools of silence, peace
Of bygone voyagers, to the close transforming pass.

Cleansed, they await, the seeker come
To a drought of centres, to slipholds on the climb

And heart may yield to strange upwelling thrusts,
Promising from far to slake immortal thirsts.

CONVERSATION AT NIGHT WITH A COCKROACH

Come out. Oh have you found me even here
Cockroach? grimed in gloss connivance
Carapaced in age, in cunning, oiled
As darkness, keyed in decoy rasps.
Your subtle feelers probed prize chapters
Drilled perforations on the magic words.
Our maps did not long survive your trails
To mislead, false contours from secretions
Of your poison ducts. Oh you have claws
To leak the day of pity, skin the night
Of love, pierce holes invisible
Within the heart of nature for all
Of good to seep through unnoticed and unmourned.
Saw teeth, dribbling a caress
Of spittle on the wound, you nibbled trust
From the heart of our concerted bond
Yet left the seals intact. Our limbs
And voices carried on to cheers and whirring
Of your fluted wings. But lost
Was the heart of purpose, soiled
Our standard of the awakened hour.

You know to wait out, sleek in dirt
The first fire-arc of regenerate eyes,
Lowered beneath the rotted roots, attuned
To a stale, complacement air. You know what hands

Are sworn to seedling, whose large Visitation
Plants even with the cropping.

Close upon their steps we creep
Cockroach, termite and train
Rooting up even before
The clutching of the germ
Foremost of the jubilating horde
Our voices lead in welcome
Below the joy-froth's endless cressets
We churn our silt of discord
And ours are fingers on the dredge
Working conveyors in reverse.
What could you? What can you?
Why do you light the fires?

In that year's crucible we sought
To force impurities in nationweal
Belly-up, heat-drawn by fires
Of truth. In that year's crucible
We sought to cleanse the faulted lodes
To raise new dwellings pillared on crags
Washed by mountain streams; to reach
Hands around Kaura hills, beyond
Obudu ranges, to dance on rockhills
Through Idanre. We sought to speak
Each to each in accents of trust
Dispersing ancient mists in clean breezes
To clear the path of lowland barriers

Forge new realities, free our earth
Of distorting shadows cast by old
And modern necromancers. No more
Rose cry and purpose, no more the fences
Of deceit, no more perpetuity
Of ancient wrongs.

But we were wise to portents, tuned
As tinsel vanes to the dread approach
Of the Visitation. And while the rumble yet
Was far, we closed, we spread the tentacles.

We knew the tread and heard
The gathering heartbeat of the cyclone heart
And quick our hands to forge coalitions new
Of tried corruptions, East to West, North to South.
Survival was insured in policies to embrace
The full degree of wavering weather vanes.
Our sirens poised inked talons on the open
Cheques, their songs inflamed each hidden longing:

Rest. Rock not our neat foundations
With futile quarrying. Pace pulses
Of your thoughts to cycles as of water-wheels
Dipping with aged ease in wells
Of milk and honey. Journeys end
On cattle hide for restless egrets
And what are desert vistas but the ruins
Of wind-blown pasts, sand-dunes

B   [7]

Of futile energies in wastrel winds
What gain the pangs of distant urges
Surge and spring of migratory power
All come at last to the placid hide
A prodigal's home-coming to the herd.

Weary? Rest, and to distant echoes of
Their evensong I'll lull you with a sweet
Lament of victims. Oh I've crept among them
Even as here, to stare and probe, seeking crumbs
Hidden or fallen. I've tickled out their dreams
With quiet antennae in the dead of night. Listen:

And we had sojourned long among
Our violators, generations of far-flung
Clans, and taken wives among them
And given daughters unto them for wives.
Our offspring knew no land but this
No air, no earth, no loves or death
Only the brittle sky in harmattan
And in due season, rain to waken scrub
A hailstone herald to the rouse
Of hills, echoes in canyons, pastures
In the palm of ranges, moss horizons
On distant ridges, anthill spires for milestones
We sought no pledges save those dusks of peace
Sung by muezzins to kith and stranger
No stranger horizon than sails of egrets
Breaking on the minarets, we walked among

Baobab landmarks on our uncharted prospects –
And this they call the tree of life! – indeed
We lived in the land of pyramids
Groundnut stacks to a skyline of the first
Exodus – there let all semblance rest –
Nor sea nor river closed upon our assailants
The plague did not plague them. Our firstborn
It was that died.

> Peace. The spillage dried with time
> We nibbled blood where it had caked
> You lit the fires, you, and saw
> Your dawn of dawning yield
> To our noon of darkness
> Half-way up your grove of union
> We watched you stumble – mere men
> Lose footing on the peaks of deities.
> The torch was quenched, the void
> Of darkness rang with madness
> Each his own priest, quick, easy
> The act of sacrifice. We know to wait.
> We nibble blood before it cakes.

Night scavengers
Heavy with the season's fruition
Whelped they in laughter
To a moon's decay

Rabid teats
To suckle rivers
A trail of slavering
Coated the whetstones
Waiting the tempering of blades

This was the dew
That fell in night hours
The night contagion

Upon new-forged weapons
In open lairs
Laid for consecration
To the love-feast of the morrow

A round table, board
Of the new abiding – man, ghoul, Cockroach,
Jackal and brood of vile cross-breedings
Broke bread to a loud veneration
Of awe-filled creatures of the wild,
Sat to a feast of love – our pulsing hearts!

Not human faces, hands, were these
That fell upon us, nor was death withheld
Even from children, from the unborn.
And wombs were torn from living women
And eyes of children taken out
On the points of knives and bayonets.
The sky was blotted out in funeral pyres

And the faggots were limbs of the living.
There was no sanctuary, in mosque or chapel,
In surgeries where we fled for healing hands,
On gravestep or in cradle. The hearses
On this day were gravel tippers, smoothly
Functioning upon the leverage of death.
An endless shuttle from rich laden fields
Of slaughter, to hasty pits, dams, ponds
Sewers. And many drew last breath
Beneath the earth, below corrupted waters.
Many, buoyed on the swollen husks
Of past departures, thrashed a dying hope
To banks. Death's face of mockery grinned
And beckoned, rock or pole in hand.
None came living from the floods
Of hate's dark waters.

    I murmured to their riven hearts:
    Yet blood must flow, a living flood
    Bravely guarded, boldly split
    A potency to rejuvenate
    Mothers-of-all earth, the river's
    Endless cycle with the sap
    Of trees, wine of palm, oil
    Of kernels, lamp-light in rock bearings
    Let even as treasures are
    An offering to red pulses
    Beating to the larger life –
    Oh I know my lore, I've heard the poets.

Stale deception. Blasphemer's consolation.
This was death in evil, death without hue
This death wore the cloak of scavengers
Grave-robbers, claws of greed on leathery hands
Blind squeaks in the humid stench
Of usurers' conservation. Death came
In the colour of foul thoughts and whispers
Fouled intentions, colour of calculations
A contrivance to erase the red and black
Of debt and credit, gangrene to discolour
Records for future reckoning, bile to blur
Precision of the mind to past exploitation
A scheming for intestate legacies
Conversions, appropriations, a mine
Of gold-filling in the teeth of death
A colour blindness to red standards
Which tomorrow shall uphold against
The horrors of today.

         They do not bleed
On whom the dunghill falls, nor they
Whose bones are sucked of marrow
In noon perversions of inhuman tongues
They do not bleed whose breaths are stilled
In sludges or sewers, who slither down
To death on the burst tumour of hate's

Inventive mind, through chasms of the flight
Of earth from rites of defilement,
Dark of abomination. They do not bleed
Whose wombs are bared to leprous lust.

Tears are rainfall in the house of death
Softening, purging, purifying. Tears
Are a watering shed to earth's
Unceasing wounds. This death was arid
There was no groan, no sorrowing at the wake –
Only curses. No suffering, for the senses
Were first to die. We died, the world
Turned a blank eye to the sky
And prayed : May Heaven comfort you;
On earth, our fears must teach us silence.

A little stone
Disgorged its tenant. The Cockroach
Spread his wings in a feeble sun
And rasped his saw-teeth. A song
Of triumph rose on deadened air
A feeler probed the awful silence,
Withdrew in foreknowing contentment –

All was well. All was even
As it was in the beginning.

A COBWEB'S TOUCH IN THE DARK

Touching
By moth-eyes on fingers, trailing
Dark vapours of the earth exhaling

Hearing
Voices of our dead in leaves their presences
Have nourished, in more than foliage essences

A skin
Whose hairs are brushed by winds that shade
Spaces where dead memories are laid

A thread
Lays its moment on the flesh, a rime
Of things gone by, a brush of time

It slips
Against the dark, radial and ebb-
line to the heart of the ancestral web.

WHEN SEASONS CHANGE

When seasons change it seems
An age is passed, and all with it
And this old earth has sucked within it
Souls of all living. Time's spectres, they
Evade guardianship of predecessors
They thread their way through rocks
And creviced growths, old, silent vapours.
What seek you, cloud weeds in air
Whose thoughts are old, hoar-rimmed
As sunken eyes on the forgotten face
Of this my hermit earth? They wander on
In whispering parade, full of old hints
Old truths upheld in mirrors of the hour –
A solemn future casts a backward glance
Over drooped shoulders.

                      The mind
Is banked upon the bankrupt flow
Of wisdoms new. It soars in flight
Upon a dual lift of planes, shifting in cross-winds
A noble slave, air-borne on the cross
Of twin-adherents, equal lift and span –
Knowledge of a deep futility in all
Of far ideas and urgent action – this
The right wing, poise and balance
Wind-drag on – the left, fate, propulsion

Beating wind and homing on the beam
Responsive ever to the present call.

Hailstone summons on the dovecot roof
The drums are here again, flight courses
Tapped on questing minds. The lines are worn
And reading blurred in time's fingerstains.
Shed your hard tears; it is an old earth
Stirring to fresh touch of old pretensions
Throbs of dead passion, chilled rebounds
From sensations of the past, old hands and voices
The blows of battle and the scars, old fences
And the guarded opening of a gate
Old welcomes, the heat of comradeship
And cold betrayal, old sacrifices
The little victories and the greater loss –
Thus, purity of ideals, clarity of vision,
And oh, let innocence have brief mourning –
Old compromises.

Yet this progression has been source
For great truths in spite of stammering
Planes for great building in spite
Of crooked sights, for plastic strength
Despite corrosive fumes of treachery
And spirits grow despite the midwifery
Of dwarfs; spires, rooted in quagmires
Of the human mind rise to purer lights
And wing aloft a salvaged essence

Transcending death, legacy of seasons . . .

Ecstasies are brief; it is truth's season
And golden eyelets sink grey hooded
In the ashen hearth of truth. Now moves
A dead recession of the silent host
Whispering judgements, sucking spires
Down to dwarf kennels, liming minds
That took to wing, sighing sinews down
To atrophy: a damp of knowing smiles
At urges of the flesh to a self-release
In transcendencies.

Shrouds of seasons gone, peeled
From time's corpses, mouse-eaten thoughts
You flutter upon solitude in winds
Armed in shrapnels from the shell of vision
Veils on the altar of unplighted troths
Cobweb hangings on the throne of death
In solitude.

TO THE MADMEN OVER THE WALL

Howl, howl
Your fill and overripeness of the heart,
I may not come with you
Companions of the broken buoy
I may not seek
The harbour of your drifting shore.

Your wise withdrawal
Who can blame? Crouched
Upon your ledge of space, do you witness
Ashes of reality drift strangely past?
I fear
Your minds have dared the infinite
And journeyed back
To speak in foreign tongues.

Though walls
May rupture tired seams
Of the magic cloak we share, yet
Closer I may not come
But though I set my ears against
The tune of setting forth, yet, howl
Upon the hour of sleep, tell these walls
The human heart may hold
Only so much despair.

I ANOINT MY FLESH
(Tenth Day Of Fast)

I anoint my flesh
Thought is hallowed in the lean
Oil of solitude
I call you forth, all, upon
Terraces of light. Let the dark
Withdraw

I anoint my voice
And let it sound hereafter
Or dissolve upon its lonely passage
In your void. Voices new
Shall rouse the echoes when
Evil shall again arise

I anoint my heart
Within its flame I lay
Spent ashes of your hate —
Let evil die.

Four archetypes

JOSEPH
(*to Mrs Potiphar*)

O Mrs Potiphar, your principles
Which I would not embrace you swore
I tried to violate; I see you wave as trophy
Tattered pieces of your masquerade
Of virtue, and call them mine.

Indeed I was not Joseph, a cursing martyr I,
No saint – are saints not moved beyond
Event, their passive valour tuned to time's
Slow unfolding? A time of evils cries
Renunciation of the saintly vision
Summons instant hands of truth to tear
All painted masks, that poison stains thereon
May join and trace the hidden undertows
In sewers of intrigue. Dear Mrs Potiphar
You seek through chaos to bury deep
Your scarlet pottage of guilt, your grim manure
For weeds of sick ambition.

                Time's slaves
Eunuchs of will wait upon you; sink
Down deep in whitened couch of bones, recline
Today upon tomorrow's hollowed skulls. We,
All whose dreams of fire resolve in light
Wait upon the old ancestor in pursuit
Of truths, and to interpret dreams.

He stilled his doubts, they rose to halt and lame
A resolution on the rack. Passion's flame
Was doused in fear of error, his mind's unease
Bred indulgence to the state's disease

Ghosts embowelled his earth; he clung to rails
In a gallery of abstractions, dissecting tales
As 'told by an idiot'. Passionless he set a stage
Of passion for the guilt he would engage.

Justice despaired. The turn and turn abouts
Of reason danced default to duty's counterpoint
Till treachery scratched the slate of primal clay
Then Metaphysics waived a thought's delay –
It took the salt in the wound, the 'point
Envenom'd too' to steel the prince of doubts.

GULLIVER

Once upon a ship-(of state)-wreck, where
The sun had shrunk the world at last to a true
Stature of deserving — the ant for unit —
I lay on earth tide-flung, obtruding
Miles of heart and mind, an alien hulk
Into a thumb assemblage. My feet
Were scaled as mountains. Fearful I was
Lest, rising, I dislodge a crossbeam
Of their skies. And this was well, I
Proved obedient to their laws: alien minds
Must learn recumbent postures. A brief
Impulse to unguided knowledge raised
A shower of needles, full-fanged, venom-bodied
I took their meaning, pressed my hands
To earth. They quenched my fleshly thirst
In draughts of Lethe, and I was plunged
Deep in mindless trance. Wheels approached,
They bore me through the famished blades —
As dead the living come into necropolis —
Corded to a span of tumbrils, drugged.

They lodged me in a hall of sorts
A desecrated temple — and this proved sign
Of much that came to pass. I schooled me
In their ways, picked a wary course
Through egg-shell structures. I looked above
Their draughty towers, peered within

Secret chambers, and marvelled at their councils.
Peacock vain, mannikin cruel, sycophant.
The world was measured to a dwarf
Sufficiency; the sun by state decree
Was lowered to fit the sextant of their mind
And planets sighted lower to turn
In calculable grooves, in orbits centred
On the palace of the Sun of suns,
Man-Mountain, King of Lilliput, Lord
And Terror of a thimble universe!

In such surrounds, in truth of fire
Was it a wonder I would sagely err?
How could a stranger tell an earthly sun
Identify as meteors matchwood tongues
Licking lawns, toy orchards, fairy groves?
In plainsight I decried an earthly burn
And squelched the puny flames in fountains
Of urine.

I sought nor favour nor reward, content
In civic duty done, presence of mind
Quick thinking. Alas! This act was rain
Upon long stunted passions,
Customs, taboos, parched sensibilities;
The storm unleashed within the chamberpot
Was long subsiding. Time passed. I kissed
The Queen's fingers. The land bestowed
A Royal Pardon. I pledged my strength anew

To service of the state, enticed the court
Statesmen, minions and nobility
To grace my temple home. They trod a measure
On the dais of my handkerchief
The king excelled in skating on a mucus
Rink – indeed we passed the rapid days
In feasts of love, in mirth and mutual service.

The seasons passed of peace, winds gathered
To a storm within an egg-cup.
Excavating scrolls in long forgotten archives
They stretched the warps of mind to rigid poles
Of opposition, blared the martial note:
From Us the Lillywhite King Lillypuss
To you obfuscating Blefuscoons
From Us the Herrenyolk of Egg
To you Albinos of the Albumen. . . . We Declare . . .!

I could not choose but serve
I took their measure in the depth
Of sea-beds, galley-slave to claims
Of bread and salt. I brought the enemy fleet
To port, and pressed a reasoned course
Of temperate victory. It did not suffice.
I pledged reversion of my strength
To arbitration; they pledged extinction of their kind.
At this rebellion of the galley slave
They looked much, said little. I waded
Home in high-tide of their hate.

[25]

Indictments flowed at secret sessions
The palace deed re-echoed, concluding –
Imprimis : Unless by aid of Secret Powers
No human bladder could eject such potent
Piss to douse sidereal flames. Thus :
Imprimis : A blasphemer who dared mistake
Cosmic conflagration for mundane disaster, and –
For paradox : An arsonist for dwarfing
Flames of Lilliput with stark reflection.

From a capital doom, the saving thought
Was waste disposal – how rid the state
Of carrion weightier than the court and state.
The Court Hygienists voiced a dread
Of plagues, infections, cautioned – Hold!
A cult of septic hydrants may derive
From such a monumental corpse, springing
To douse orthodoxies of state and power
In rank corrosive draughts! A compromise
Was sought and found, the sentence writ :

The fault is not in ill-will but in seeing ill
The drab-horse labours best with blinkers
We pardon him to lose his sight to a cure
Of heated needles, that proven cure for all
Abnormalities of view – foresight, insight
Second sight and all solecisms of seeing –

Called vision.

ULYSSES
Notes from here to my Joyce class

Haunting the music of the mind, I watched
Once, through sun slats, a raindrop
Lengthen out to rivers on a window-pane
And on this painless rack of time, stretched
I was, heritage of thought, clay and voices
Passing easily to wind and rain-becoming
And, lest I lose the landmarks of my being
Pocked the air with terse, echoing rounds
Drumtap feelers on the growth of leaves.

This storm has cold wings, and they beat
An interchange in time to death and birth
The rain's harrowing passion, midwife love
Winds newcomer-wanderer in its toils.
Lodged in barenness of ante-rooms
To manger-haven, I, sleep-walker through
The weary cycle of the season's womb
Labouring to give birth to her deathless self,
One more reveller at the rites, I watch
The years re-lay their yeasting dregs
Beneath the froth, hard soles travel pressed
In poultice of new loam. We embrace,
The world and I in great infinitudes.
I grow into that portion of the world
Lapping my feet, yet bear the rain of nails

[27]

That drill within to the archetypal heart
Of all lone wanderers.

How pleasant to have toyed with concepts.
Time – we touched upon it – Time I hold
Beyond my hands, a febrile heart slowing
To the calm of death. It weighs all and nothing,
Ceased with rain and ran between my fingers.
It was a crystal cover on the world
A rake of thunders showered its fragments
To a slow dissolve in hailstones, and I was
Held awhile to its truthfulness of transience.
But not for long. It flowed to raise a flotsam from
Tobacco shreds, weaving space inflated
To a swell of dancing seas and pygmy fountains –
Detritus of change, warts on continuity
Drowned steeples of the broken sees, tossed thorn
In matriseas – mud consummation. I trail
A sea-weed cord to hold your breaths to mine
Prime turd among a sea of faeces – oh how
We surf-wrestle to manure the land at ebb!
How golden finally is the recovered fleece?
A question we refuse to ask the Bard.

It turns on quest cycles, to track a skein
Of self through eyeless veils, stumble on warps
Endure the blinds of spidery distortions, till
Swine-scented folds and caressing tunnels
Come to crossroads at the straits, between

Vaginal rocks. Here, the moment of time's
Overlap, forfeiture of flesh, we shed
Our questions, here, turn from bridging
Passes of eroded runs, from scratching
Upon the calloused skin of blind redemptive
Doors. On minds grown hoary from the quest
Rest, rooted even in the turmoil agency
A boulder solitude amidst wine-centred waves
And hold, in paradox of lighthouse windows
On dark-fallen seas, our lighted beings
Suspended as mirages on the world's reality.

Chimes of Silence

At first there is a peep-hole on the living.

It sneaks into the yard of lunatics, lifers, violent and violated nerves, cripples, tuberculars, victims of power sadism safely hidden from questions. A little square hole cut in the door, enough for a gaoler's fist to pass through and manipulate the bolt from either side. Enough also for me to – casually, oh so casually – steal a quick look at the rare flash of a hand, a face, a gesture; more often a blur of khaki, the square planted rear of the guard on the other side.

Until one day, a noise of hammering. All morning an assault of blows multiplied and magnified by the unique echoing powers of my crypt. (When it thunders, my skull *is* the anvil of gods.) By noon that breach is sealed. Only the sky is now open, a sky the size of a napkin trapped by tall spikes and broken bottles, but a sky. Vultures perch on a roof just visible from another yard. And crows. Egrets overfly my crypt and bats swarm at sunset. Albino bats, sickly pale, emitting radio pips to prowl the echo chamber. But the world is dead, suddenly. For an eternity after ceasing the hammers sustain their vehemence. Even the sky retracts, dead.

Buried alive? No. Only something men read of. Buoys and landmarks vanish. Slowly, remorselessly, reality dissolves and certitude betrays the mind.

Days weeks months, then as suddenly as that first death, a new sound, a procession. Feet approach, dragging to the clank of chains. And now another breach that has long remained in-

[31]

different, blank, a floodhole cut in the base of the wall, this emptiness slowly, gracelessly, begins to frame manacled feet. Nothing has ever passed so close, so ponderously across the floodhole of the Wailing Wall. (I named it that, because it overlooks the yard where a voice cried out in agony all of one night and died at dawn, unattended. It is the yard from which hymns and prayers rise with a constancy matched only by the vigil of crows and vultures.) And now, feet. Bare except for two pairs of boots which consciously walk deadweight to match the pace of manacles on the others. Towards noon the same procession passes the other way. Some days later the procession again goes by and I count. Eleven. The third day of this procession wakes into the longest dawn that ever was born and died of silence, a silence replete and awesome. My counting stops brusquely at six. No more. In that instant the ritual is laid bare, the silence, the furtive conspiracy of dawn, the muffled secrets hammer louder than manacles in my head, all all is bared in one paralysing understanding. Five men are walking the other way, five men walking even more slowly, wearily, with the weight of the world on each foot, on each step towards eternity. I hear them pause at every scrap of life, at every beat of the silence, at every mote in the sun, those five for whom the world is about to die.

Sounds. Sounds acquire a fourth dimension in a living crypt. A definition which, as in the case of thunder becomes physically unbearable. In the case of the awaited but unheard, psychically punishing. Pips from albino bats pock the babble of evensong – moslem and christian, pagan and unclassifiable. My crypt they

[32]

turn into a cauldron, an inverted bell of faiths whose sonorities are gathered, stirred, skimmed, sieved in the warp and weft of sooty mildew on walls, of green velvet fungus woven by the rain's cunning fingers. From beyond the Wall of Mists the perverse piety of women, that inhuman patience to which they are born drifts across to lash the anguish from the Wall of Purgatory. A clap of wings – a white-and-ochre bolt, a wood-pigeon diving and crossing, a restless shuttle threading sun-patches through this darkest of looms. Beyond and above the outside wall, a rustle of leaves – a boy's face! A guileless hunter unmasks, in innocence – an evil labyrinth. I shall know his voice when children's songs invade the cauldron of sounds at twilight, this pulse intrusion in the home of death.

The sun is rising behind him. His head dissolves in the pool, a shuttle sinking in a fiery loom.

I   *Wailing Wall*

Wall to polar star, wall of prayers
A roof in blood-rust floats beyond
Stained-glass wounds on wailing walls
Vulture presides in tattered surplice
In schism for collection plates, with –

Crow in white collar, legs
Of toothpick dearth plunged
Deep in a salvaged morsel. Choirmaster
When a hymn is called he conducts,
Baton-beaking their massed discordance:
Invocation to the broken Word
On broken voices

    Air-tramp, black verger
    Descend on dry prayers
    To altars of evil
    And a charity of victims

On your raft of faith, calling
Darkest dawn to nightfall
I fear in vain you exorcise the past
For evil is impenitent, evil feeds
Upon the wounds and tears of piety

O Wall of prayers, preyed upon
By scavenger, undertaker.

Nightly the Plough
Furrows deep in graveyards of the sky
For a mass burial
Before the lowering poised
A long low coffin of the roof
Bulks against the sky –
Glow of mourning candles in far spaces

Cloud drifts across the Plough
The share is sunk, and hope
Buried in soil of darkness.

II   *Wall of Mists*

Wall of mists, wall of echoes
High pitch, shrill laughter
They feed no fires, prompt no pains
Wake no memories : walls
Are the tomb of longing

Witches' Sabbath what you hold
Vermilion lizards in sun orgies
Monster beetles in wall ulcers, broiled
In steam of mildew drying

Mists of metamorphosis
Men to swine, strength to blows
Grace to lizard prances, honour
To sweetmeats on the tongue of vileness

There rose a shrillness in the air
Grunts, squeals, cackles, wheezes
Remainder membranes of once human throats
A thundercrack in air – the whip
Of Circe calling home her flock
Of transformations?

And echoes roam of disembodied laughter
Borne on soiled streams, sound-waves
On maze of underwall gutters
Brown waters, the lost and dispossessed
Flow beneath my feet, flotsam of the living dead
Dark channels, link of all bereaved.

Pale bats at twilight
Rank incense to efface the sun
A dark of shifting shadows
Vapours of the purple paste
Of sunset.

Breath of the sun, crowned
In green crepes and amber beads
Children's voices at the door of Orient

Raising eyelids on the sluggish earth
Dispersing sulphur fumes above the lake
Of awakening, you come hunting with the sun

His hands upon the loftiest branches
Halted on the prize, eyes in wonderlust
Questioned this mystery of man's isolation

Fantasies richer than burning mangoes
Flickered through his royal mind, an open
Noon above the door that closed

I would you may discover, mid-morning
To the man's estate, with lesser pain
The wall of gain within the outer loss

Your flutes at evening, your seed-awakening
Dances fill the night with growth; I hear
The sun's sad chorus to your starlit songs

Wall of flagellation to the South
Strokes of justice slice a festive air –
It is the day of reckoning

In puppet cast: first, by law compelled
The surgeon, either primed for the ordeal
Next, a cardboard row of gaolers, eyelids
Of glue – the observation squad. And:
Hero of the piece, a towering shade across
The prostrate villain, cuts a trial swathe
In air, nostalgic for the thumbscrew
Rack and nail extractors – alas, all
Good things shall pass away – he adapts
To the regulation cane. Stage props:
Bench for a naked body, crusted towel,
Pail of antiseptic yellow to impart
Wet timbres to dry measures of the Law.

>   The circus comes to circus town
>   A freak show comes to freaks
>   An ancient pageant to divert
>   Archetypes of Purgatorio

For here the mad commingle with the damned.
Epileptics, seers and visionaries
Addicts of unknown addictions, soulmates
To the vegetable soul, and grey

Companions to the ghosts of landmarks
Trudging the lifelong road to a dread
Judicial sentence

And some have walked to the edge of the valley
Of the shadow; and, at a faint stir in memories
Long faded to the moment of the miracle of reprieve
To a knowledge of rebirth and a promise of tomorrows
And tomorrows and an ever beginning of tomorrows
The mind retreats behind a calloused shelter
Of walls, self-censor on the freedom of remembrance
Tempering visions to opaque masonry, to rings
Of iron spikes, a peace of refuge passionless
And comfort of a gelded sanity.

Weaned from the moment of death, the miracle
Dulled, their minds dissolve in vagueness, a look
Empty as all thoughts are featureless which
Plunge to that lone abyss – And
Had it there ended? Had it all ended, there
Even in the valley of the shadow of Night?

V   *Vault Centre*

I

        Corpse of Vault Centre and the lone
        Wood-pigeons breast my ghostly thoughts
D   [39]

On swelling prows of down, plunge
To grass-roots, soar to fountains of the sun

League of sun-gleaners, coursers
On golden chutes, air-gliders feather-vain
On wind-currents, you have fed –
Richer than ravens bald Elijah,

With arcs and eights, death-dives
And love-duets, frilled parabolas
Curved beams and vaulting on my air-ceiling –
This still centre of our compass points.

II

A choir of egrets, servers at the day's
Recessional, on aisles fading to the infinite

Standard bearers of twilight, pride
Of sky-order, coasting homeward with the sun

Bearing vespers from the wall of prayers
To gods unknown, altar-cloths of dusk

Host of communion wafers to dissolve
Within the closing lips of day

My quiver empties to the eternal quest
A needle's glimmer in the emptiness of night

The day's sift filters down
And I, a shawl of grey repose
Fine moves of air, gather dusks in me
An oriel window, eye on chapel ruins.

PROCESSION

I

Hanging day. A hollow earth
Echoes footsteps of the grave procession
Walls in sunspots
Lean to shadows of the shortening morn

Behind, an eyepatch lushly blue.
The wall of prayer has taken refuge
In a peace of blindness, closed
Its grey recessive deeps. Fretful limbs

And glances that would sometimes
Conjure up a drawbridge
Raised but never lowered between
Their gathering and my sway

Withdraw, as all the living world
Belie their absence in a feel of eyes
Barred and secret in the empty home

[41]

Of shuttered windows. I know the heart
Has journeyed far from present

Tread. Drop. Dread Drop. Dead

What may I tell you? What reveal?
I who before them peered unseen
Who stood one-legged on the untrodden
Verge — lest I should not return.

That I received them? That I
Wheeled above and flew beneath them
And brought them on their way
And came to mine, even to the edge
Of the unspeakable encirclement?
What may I tell you of the five
Bell-ringers on the ropes to chimes
Of silence?
What tell you of rigors of the law?
From watchtowers on stunted walls,
Raised to stay a siege of darkness
What whisper to their football thunders
Vanishing to shrouds of sunlight?

Let no man speak of justice, guilt.
Far away, blood-stained in their
Tens of thousands, hands that damned
These wretches to the pit triumph
But here, alone the solitary deed.

[42]

Passage. Earth is rich in rotteness of things
A soothing tang of compost filters
Through yeasting seeds, rain-sodden
And festive fermentation, a sweetness
Velvety as mead and maggots

Shade your sight from glare
Of leavings on the mound. The feast is done.
A coil of cigarette ribbon recreates
A violet question on the refuse heap
A headless serpent arched in fire
In vibrancy of tinsel light, winding
To futile answers, barren knowledge.

Passage. A finite step is turned
Aside to spare a bean-cake hive, swarm
Of ant-foragers – do not these
Hold a vital motion of earth?
Grooves in bean-cake scored
With identations of the carious greed
Of priesthood – how well we know them –
Inheritors of the stricken hearth.

Their hands are closed on emptiness
And opening, shall give nothing out.
Cast your eyes from leavings on the mound

Moulting in the sun, from loosened teeth whose harvest
Plagues the world in serpents.

Passage. A streak of earth on whitewashed stones –
Ghosts. Here old women spat their frail
Sibilant juice, and time was essence
Of the bitter nut seeping from withered gums,
We took their love. Through intertwine
Of owlish fingers on the loom, they gave
And wove a spell against this hour
And kept a vigil upon dearth and death.

The feast is done. See where they pass
Our old women of the loom, and they bring
On silent feet schoes in moult of earth
Indigo shawls filled with burrs of night
We lean forward to a drift of dirges
Reconciled in song to passing over
Across the mortar of fire. A pool
Hanging on the mortar's underside
Stays the folded shuttle of the loom.

Passage. Straits of mildew narrowing
To a doorless barrier of light
This is the last we shall revisit
Passageways of childhood, through rows
Of broadlooms weaving emerald tapestries
To wind the effigy of changing seasons
To move again in quest of fear,

Recall the leathern dark of bats – that
Was shadow of ill they said. Did we pass under?
By day it hung a deathness over all
It froze the sunlight in the flight
Of weavers' hands, lowering portents
In shadow humps, pressing from fig branches.

If you pass under, trap a sky-soul bird
Your foot upon its shadow as it flies.

In the passage of looms, to a hum
Of water rising in dark wells
There to play at trap-the-shuttle
To step on the flight of its shadow-soul
And hold it captive in a home
Of air and threadwaves, a lamp
Of dye-fuels hissing in the sun
Elusive as the thread's design.

By footfall on the shade of wings
On earth, a bird may drop as rain.

Ghost fires, loom whispers, indigo lines
On the broad palm of the loom
Web of air-roots falling into silence
Watching the bird that drops as rain
By a hermit's footfall on the wings

Tread Drop Dread Drop Dead

Spiralled on the unseen beam
Pall-bearer to hereafter, I attend.
Mine the bedraggled wings
Raising a wind's lament to every step
Floating on lakes to cries of drowning
Where pebbles bask in twilights of departing,
Mellowed by the sun's last whispers.

Waiting for a sound that never comes
To footfalls long receded, echoing
In craters newly opened into space
Listening to a falter of feet
Upon the dark threshold.

LAST TURNING

the last among the five

This is the last turning of the road
Around this rockface, self
Encounters self, turn pilgrim now
Into souls' kingdom

This is the last turning of the road
Nature's time-passing tales have gathered
Puns, fables, riddles of the lone
In your passage embodied

Bronzed in seasons of your journeying
Guarded by storms, lulled in earthquake
Pathways narrow on the mountain-top
A sheath for the wanderer

Fingers of thorn on stony hill
Passionate gleaner, a path of weeds
Comes to time's orchard – on beds of vines
Press lenten hands

Shaded by wings of silence, dark
Tapestries of time's unfading imprints
Where the peaks' fine needles have embossed
Missals on the heart

[47]

Read therein the earth in tremor
Pierce the day's elusive blindfold
Drink clear-headed of the Night's
Enlightening potion

Whose feet wear companion blisters
To the weathered face of cliffs
Whose night-webbed hands have closed upon
Death's awesome silence

And your companion dead, fallen
On hillside, all were steps on the ascent
Parts to the sum of seekers' questions
Sandals on milestones

Linked by drops shared in evil
To a chrysalis of cairns shall come
Rain's awakening, to heirs of sandals
Waters of insight

Into this last turning, pilgrim
Turn alone and bid you welcome
Into this last kingdom, king
Priest, and subject.

RECESSION *(Mahapralaya*)*

welcome o black dawn
whirl-winged, coeval chimes
marsh-glow of origin, dark
of night's ingestion, welcome
union of flame and seal

into the backward reel of time
the heartwood-proud towers, sinking
have folded down their palanquins
the bowers are indrawn
to the forgotten seed

i woke to bells of dreaded nuptials
to a rumble of wheels in baptismal fonts
a song of cyclones in silence of shells
the dew departing to primacy of waters

i woke egret-breasted to a peace of fire
to a shudder of earth in cavalcades of dawn
blinded at last in a rouse of ashes
i move to a dark of insight – it is time

a carillon of wings in shuttered steeples
ropes to communion bells descend to roots
toll for the last dawn, sink spire, sink light
to ancestry of seed, to the dark-in-being

* In Hindu Metaphysics, the return of the universe to its womb; here,
expressed as the consoling experience of man in the moment of death,
the freeing of his being from the death of the world.

[49]

the stems of springs are broken, the unplaced source
turned from fountains and watering of growth
folded to the long sleep of waters, brides on a bed of germ
in the unbroken seed

cliffs of clay have walled the human pass
a lifelong fall of ash has sealed the straits
now flares the savaged ember
now lifts the pinioned egret through the pass

breasting the backward drift of hours
the heights are parted to the stress of wings
and his the final argosy, white courier
free, the impenetrable moiety

homing to purify space of measure
lodestone of star courses, turning
belts on the home voyage of planets
navel of apocalyptic tides. . . .

a spring is touched by appointed fingers

and whirlwings fold into the dark
a glacier mind of all-being
slows to a last enduring thought
a deadweight seal of silence sways
upon the secret — at this wake

none keeps vigil. none.

[50]

HUNT OF THE STONE*

*interlude for the meteor that plunged earthwards
months later, and fell – within the hanging yard?*

Where lightning heads collide, and
A blot of darkness breaks and traces
Landscapes of the banished heart, there
Too instant for the rain's reflecting lakes
A form is poised, and folding
Sinks to a labyrinth of doubts

To a lure of thunderstones mortal ears
Are tuned, seeking, they know not why
Except as lodestones point to meeting-place
They turn to poles of space.

And a garbage heap may hold, sealed
In tunnel of its fiery violation
A primeval shrine, a searing run
In chambers of immortal silence
As dark unholy surfeits

Shape the clean ascetic silo
Long travelled in dimensions of the loom
The bird of pressed wings may come to rest
The tapestry of cycles, rolled
And hoarded to a chosen germ

Within the silent sentinel, may wake
To lonely chimes of rain

Thrust from a spyhole writhes
The unleavened agent, dumb and blinded,
The stone has taken vengeance on the dare
Of perjured eyes, and he was balked
Razed and shattered, bared
To the awesome rhapsody of light.

Priest and acolyte, swinge of incense
At the barrier of immanence –
Homage of clay hearts. Frail
Their fingers tend the weaker flame
But they hover, full of evil rites
To trap the frozen lake of distant fires
In walls of hate and terror.

Ants in their own teeth grooving
They scurry, their hands
Closing ever upon emptiness

They cast their ring of spells around
The ruined hermitage of the Visitation
In a bed of ash, sheltered in lowly beams
Hidden from world-weal and death depression
A nestling glow, the slumbering centre
Of the universe

They asked this hermit but he would not know
His outer blindness looked within their guise
His foot was gentle on the flow of wings
Waiting, peaceful in passage of the looms.

A gleam among the rubble, a coral eye
Watchful on passage. Priest-scavengers
All shall lose their way, their hands
Shall close on emptiness, even their cunning
Fingers of brass. They shall hold
Nought but husks of the seed of passage, though
They sift in ashes of eternity. The shuttle-eel
Shall their nets escape though they cast
In waters of the Deluge.

* When lightning strikes the priests of Sango god of thunder hunt for
the stone and take possession of the gods of the stricken house,
doubly impoverishing the unfortunate inmates. There is a myth also
that Sango strikes down malefactors or their homes. In whatever case
the priests profit, first by the magical resources of the 'stone' and then
by the forfeited goods.

SPACE

His mind was boundless when out
He flew, he was a true-cast silence
On air and water manifold
Thrust from the matrix of an ark

Breath of light, weaver-wings in loom
Of the immeasurable, from cusp
Of praying hands parted to redeem
Pledges of the first, unbroken Fiat

He flies to test the deluge for a straw
Fording the shrouded estuary of wrath
Courier from caulk and roof of the favoured
Flotsam, one among the perished all

Through webs of fireflies he drove
A gentle wedge in sapwood of the sky
As true as pilgrim comes to springs
Homed the white shadow on the loom

His plenitude a white tent laid
On cobalt sands, and he, forecourser —
Lest the flood cycles be forgot —
Plucks the caravan a date. The stone

The heartstone source of true mirages
Opens to a fiery oasis on the East

Wingless if flew, incense-boat inlaid
With currents of hope, a quiver of mist
Dipping to a bodiless song of air
An oval robe of moonlight paling
A period luminous with silence, drawn
To ghost fingers on the enamoured loom

Between the outward journey and the glance
Backward to a glaze of surfaces before
Untenanted, he saw – newsprung
Dust interstices to measure space!

Is it a wonder he will not return?
He seeks his rest on crosswinds
Emptying to one inchoate flux
Eternal deluge of a Word's design!

SEED

Roll away the stone to echoes
Of silver reins retreating. Wash ears
Of corn in rain to await dawn's embassy
Unshroud the cavern's other mouth
Where Lazarus sheds his rags and tears.

Hour of kernel-baiting
Hour of wrestling dreams awake
Splitting wood-grains to reveal
The hoard of time from passages of fear
Seeking womb-fruit lest it sink again
In tepid ash.

Light the old hearths
With salt and oil, with tubers
Camwood, chalk and antimony
What will they tell us, these
Dark ancestors of the doom?

I speak in the voice of gentle rain
In whispers of growth
In sleight of light
I speak in aged hairs of wind
Midwife to cloud
And sheaves on threshing-floor

I speak in the tread of waters
In fingers of thatch
In veined palm of the unseen guest
Pressing on roof for admittance

I wait on the winnowing run
Of breezes, on songs gathered
To green ears in a field of sap
I wait on footpads of the rain

I waited on the sonorous sift
Of ashes, and I was plucked
As tendril strings by questers' fingers
Rhymed to notations of ebony rings

I fold as rings
Falling from silence of petrified years
To animystic moments of all sleep
Counted in grains of sand or wood
Into whose perfumed bosom we shall drop

As heavy worlds, gather
As grains in full-sap weaving of the field
To winds of passage

Drop, as moments, dissolve
In solitudes of dark ebony essence
Dirge, loom, emptiness of passage.

[57]

Prisonnettes

The form was quite arbitrary, something short enough and as self-containing as possible to remain in the head until, at night-time or in a slack moment of surveillance I could transfer it to the inside of a cigarette packet or an equally precious scrap of salvage. The verses naturally belong to several groups, perhaps the only two that require comment being (1) the 'cursifying' or letting-out-rage genre, of whose efficacy let no man stand in doubt, and (2) the so-called Animystic spells which induced a state of self-hypnosis (by constant repetition, accompanied by a mental pacing of the images, an attempt so to speak, to hold and follow through such images in the mind as the words are muttered). The result – a state of weightlessness etc. etc. familiar enough to those who dabble in the more esoteric religions. Both acted as counter to each other: in such situations it is easy to be self-destructively violent (internally) as to be self-destructively quiescent and forgiving.

The prisonnettes are dedicated to all who participated in the two-year experiment on how to break down the human mind. (Including of course those who gave the orders.)

LIVE BURIAL

Sixteen paces
By twenty-three. They hold
Siege against humanity
And Truth
Employing time to drill through to his sanity

Schismatic
Lover of Antigone!
You will? You will unearth
Corpses of yester-
Year? Expose manure of present birth?

Seal him live
In that same necropolis.
May his ghost mistress
Point the classic
Route to Outsiders' Stygian Mysteries.

Bulletin:
He sleeps well, eats
Well. His doctors note
No damage
Our plastic surgeons tend his public image.

Confession
Fiction? Is truth not essence
Of Art, and fiction Art?

Lest it rust
We kindly borrowed his poetic licence.

Galileo
We hoped he'd prove – age
Or genius may recant – our butchers
Tired of waiting
Ordered; take the scapegoat, drop the sage.

Guards The lizard:
Every minute scrapes
A concrete mixer throat.
The cola slime
Flies to blotch the walls in patterned grime

The ghoul:
Flushed from hanging, sniffles
Snuff, to clear his head of
Sins – the law
Declared – that morning's gallows load were dead of.

The voyeur:
Times his sly patrol
For the hour upon the throne
I think he thrills
To hear the Muse's constipated groan

FLOWERS FOR MY LAND

From a distant
Shore they cry, Where
Are all the flowers gone?
I cannot tell
The gardens here are furrowed still and bare.

Death alike
We sow. Each novel horror
Whets inhuman appetites
I do not
Dare to think these bones will bloom tomorrow

Garlands
Of scavengers weigh
Heavy on human breasts
Such
Are flowers that fill the garden of decay

Seeking:
Voices of rain in sunshine
Blue kites on ivory-cloud
Towers
Smell of passing hands on mountain flowers

I saw:
Four steel kites, riders
On shrouded towers

Do you think
Their arms are spread to scatter mountain flowers?

Seeking: Truth
Seeds split and browse
In ordure, corruption. From
Beds of worms
Ivory towers uphold the charnel-house

I know
Of flowers unseen, and they
Distil beatific dawns
But tares
Withhold possession of our mangled lawns

Visions pall
Realities invade
Our innermost sanctuaries
Oil erupts
Upon the altar, casts an evil shade

Hooded hands
Knock upon our doors
We say, let them have place
And offer
Ours in hope to make a common cause

It cannot be!
Hands of slag, fingers

[63]

Of spike, they press to full
Possession.
Creepers, climbers thrive beneath their rule

Slogans
Louder than empty barrels
And more barren, a rattle
In cups of beggary
Monkeys in livery dance to barrel organs

Break who can
The yet encroaching ring
Their hands are tainted, their breath
Withers all
They feed their thoughts upon the bounty of death

I traced
A dew-lane on the sun-
flower leaf; a hailstone
Burning, blew
A trap-door on my lane for falling through

These buds
That burst upon our prayers
Diffuse an equal essence
Will for ill
As others their atomic efflorescence

Alienates
Of heart from land, outcasts
Of toadstool blooms, the coral
Is a grim
Historic flower, a now and future moral

Come, let us
With that mangled kind
Make pact, no less
Against the lesser
Leagues of death, and mutilators of the mind.

Take Justice
In your hands who can
Or dare. Insensate sword
Of Power
Outherods Herod and the law's outlawed

Sun-beacons
On every darkened shore
Orphans of the world
Ignite! Draw
Your fuel of pain from earth's sated core.

ANIMYSTIC SPELLS

I

First you must
Walk among the faceless
Their feet are shod in earth
And dung
Caryatids in anterooms of night's inbirth

Shards strewn
On secret passages of night
Their creviced skin is dew
Inlaid, star-wells
For nights of drought, for dearth of light

Hold
As they, bread as breath
Is held and spent, discarding
Weights of time
In clutching and possessing – yokes of death.

The quest
Is all, endless
The home-coming
Respite
Before the gathering of the outward crest

II

Eyes
That grow as stamens need
A yeast of pollen. Shun
Visions
Of the unleavened, look sooner on the sun.

III

Death
Embraces you and I
A twilight cone is
Meeting-place
The silent junction of the grey abyss

IV

The past
Dissolves in lacquered notes
Lips on woodwind, ears
Of grain
Swaying to echoes in a veil of rust

V

Incense
Of pines when a page
Is turned, woodsmoke
Rings
Across a thousand years to a bygone sage

VI

Fragments
We cannot hold, linger
Parings of intuition
Footsteps
Passing and re-passing the door of recognition

VII

Line
Of the withered bough
Hill and broken valleys
Dearth
On thirsty palm to furrows of the earth

VIII

Blood
When it is done – dearth
Of lines from palm to love
Light,
Springs, to patient wrinkles of the earth

IX

Links
Of dust, Whitened rib
Of ghosts to flute
Home-coming
Moth-fingers hover on the new-laid crib

Three millet
Stalks. A tasselled crown
On a broken glass horizon
Weeds clogged
Their feet, winds came and blew them down

New ears arose
Lean lances through
A stubbed and mangled mound –
And this I saw –
Their grains were ripened closer to the ground.

BACKGROUND AND FRIEZES

They varied Death
A thousand ways – sudden
To piecemeal. Virgins bled
At lepers' orgies
The streets were cobbled with unnumbered dead

Jacques d'Odan
Wise angel not to rush
Where no hero treads
Whispers – stop!
This spree is getting out of hand – and heads

Rinses
Clean fingers in a bowl
Of blood, and humbly adds
Pips and crowns
To a General make-weight of his shoulder-pads

My word
Is bond. Whom I treat
To the sworn safe-conduct
I guarantee
Will journey safely down the one-way street

Street singers
Chant my tune: I am
God's chosen instrument

Do I hear –
Played upon by fat unholy fingers?

Boots? Butts?
Only a mild reproach
He lives, a mud reptilian
Heed sirens!
Drive into the sea at my approach!

Humane
My code of conduct, creed
Of good intentions, gun-mate
Cromwellian style
Some day we'll teach the soldiery to read

Hands off!
My affair's internal
Await my beggar's cup
For when I'm sated
Me to burn, you to grant full aid eternal

A beach
Hides the pebble. Create –
But bleach (or whitewash) –
Cairns
Of bones to hide the skeleton of hate

Futile shield
Before the festive slayers

F*   [73]

Mother to child, prayers
Unavailing
The scene is old, cue in the waiting players

Week Seventy-five:
Observers welcome. Cheap
Conducted tours – behold!
Our hands are clean.
The rains have fallen twice and earth is deep.

FUTURE PLANS

The meeting is called
To odium : Forgers, framers
Fabricators Inter-
national. Chairman,
A dark horse, a circus nag turned blinkered sprinter

Mach Three
We rate him – one for the Knife
Two for 'iavelli, Three –
Breaking speed
Of the truth barrier by a swooping detention decree

Projects in view :
Mao Tse Tung in league
With Chiang Kai. Nkrumah
Makes a secret
Pact with Verwood, sworn by Hastings Banda.

Proven : Arafat
In flagrante cum
Golda Meir. Castro drunk
With Richard Nixon
Contraceptives stacked beneath the papal bunk . . .

. . . and more to come

Poems of bread and earth

RELIEF

Or, Wedding in a Minor Key

Bread is magic, grace.
Some touch the whitefluff only
With crested silver spoon
With coat of arms
And liveried service. Delicately.
Bread is magic, grace. *Your* grace
Is not the pulse of life,
Your Grace.

Bread is magic, grace.
The mouldy crust alone was life and pulse
Dungbread, blackbread, wholebread, rankbread
Sparebreadstockbreadgutbreadbloodandsweatbread –
BREAD!!! was that the victims craved
Locked so long with hate and fear
And fire before their eyes.

When he had
Dined and wined and – surely – wived. . . .
And much human dough there was
Broken round his board and court
Around his state and splendour. . . .
When he had
Dined and wined, and strutted wiving-poised
He ordered:

Empty that plane
Of bread, damn bread! Turn its nose
To a different wind, to a perfumed wind
Fill the hold with cake and wine
And champagne guests – It's time
For MY wedding. And –
Shut those hungry mouths! – I have
Good Precedent.

CAPITAL

It cannot be
That germ which earth has nurtured
Man tended – once I watched a waterfall
Of germ, a grain-spray plenitude
Belched from chutes of wide-mouthed
Glad satiation; I swear the grains
Were singing –

It cannot be
That policy, deliberation
Turns these embers of my life
To ashes, and in polluted seas
Lay sad beds of yeast to raise
Dough
On the world market.

UJAMAA

(for Julius Nyerere)

Sweat is leaven for the earth
Not tribute. Earth replete
Seeks no homage from the toil of earth.
Sweat is leaven for the earth
Not driven homage to a fortressed god.
Your black earth hands unchain
Hope from death messengers, from
In-bred dogmanoids that prove
Grimmer than the Grim Reaper, insatiate
Predators on humanity, their fodder.
Sweat is leaven, bread, Ujamaa
Bread of the earth, by the earth
For the earth. Earth is all people.

EVER-READY BANK ACCOUNTS

Ever-ready bank accounts
Are ever red
Cash may be set on paper, all it reads
Is – Bread Bread Bread! Among a thousand fingers
Clutching loud at plenty, arms
Stacked too full of loaves cannot
Embrace mankind. Ever-ready bank accounts
Are never read where
Children slay the cockroach for a meal
Awaiting father-forager's return
The mind of hungered innocence must turn
To strange cuisine – kebab of houseflies
On a broomstick prong; beetles broiled in carapace
Slugs are scientific stores of high protein –
They tell me – I never tried it yet.
Awaiting father-forager's return with empty sack
He went and came that way these two-year gone
He will tomorrow . . .

                I take the folded statement
Slipped below the grill. Discreetly. Below the solemn
Chiding glare of my good friend and foe
The bank clerk, the white-shirt guardian of the vaults
Of paper, mystic signs, those noughts and crosses
Which I bear – the language of his statement reads :
Charity may be a one-way street, it's not
A one-man way of life. And like the ink
It's printed on, I go red beneath

My black deceit, my bold and knowing
"Damn-they're-late-again-with-that-cheque skin –
You know, my royalties, late again I see
It's alright really, do present it at month's end"
Cursing the last extortion I was guilty of
For falling prey to. I have observed it –
The latest cup of supplicating hands is always
Drier than the last. And rats are sleeker now
Whose raw-eyed thrusts dispute
Crumbs with new-hatched mouths of want. . . .

Now that was long ago, and yesterday, and Now
The longer statement trails a longer line
Of bread, and now again that mournful statement
Marred by sceptic stares – but HE we know,
He earns the sky, commands a fortune when he farts
And all it reads is that one line, one ledgered statement –
Charity may be a one-way street, it's not
A one-man way of life – Your balance sir
Your balance is that figure etched in red. . . .

A page, a ready reddening reckoner falls open on
The seven-year lease on seven-floor heights
Of the seventh wonder of a pocket world
The seventh wonder of the seven-year plan of lies
Seven times grander than the last grandiose deceit.

Justify the seven-year lease on seven-floor heights:
"I'd live there if I could. I built that

Seven-tiered modest monster for a home
But duties of the seven-year plan demand
My absence thence, and how may seven-year seeds
Not yield a modest sevenfold green return?"

A balance sheet is waved, a flag on stolen heights
And who goes red invisibly beneath their black deceit?
A balance sheet is hung in rags on barren trees
And who turns red invisibly beneath their black despair?
And who turns red for who turns red, and who turns when

To light, across that broken road a fire that heals
From logs whose weight upon a great
Grandmother arched in pain still shapes —
A loaded question mark?

APRES LA GUERRE

Do not cover up the scars
In the quick distillery of blood
I have smelt
Seepage from familiar opiates,
Do not cover up the scars

The tuber of our common flesh, when
Trampled deep in earth embattles
Death, new-girthed, lunges at the sun
But lest it prove a hollowed shell
And lest the feet of new-born lives
Sink in voids of counterfeiting
Do not swell earth's broken skin
To glaze the fissures in the drum

Do not cover up with scabs
And turn the pain a masquerader's
Broken-tongued lament
Its face a painted mask of veils
Its breath unmoistened by the run of bile
A patchwork heart and death-head grin
To cheat the rigors of
Exorcism.

Paint cracks. Bequeath
The heartwood beat alone
To new-born
Followers of the wake.

[84]

JOURNEY

I never feel I have arrived, though I come
To journey's end. I took the road
That loses crest to questions, yet bears me
Down the other homeward earth. I know
My flesh is nibbled clean, lost
To fretful fish among the rusted hulls –
I passed them on my way

And so with bread and wine
I lack the sharing with defeat and dearth
I passed them on my way.

I never feel I have arrived
Though love and welcome snare me home
Usurpers hand my cup at every
Feast a last supper

Epilogue

AND WHAT OF IT IF THUS HE DIED?

for Victor Banjo
And for George Jackson
And All, All, All

Not that he loved sunrise less
But truly, as love's caress
Whose craving must to spring devices lead.

Nor deaf nor blind lived he
To beauty's promise, to laughter
In light hours, but these he sought
To seal and to perpetuate
Upon the face of dearth.

Knowledge was not a golden plate
For feasts at the board of privilege
But a trowel laid to deep foundations
In sighted fingers of a master mason.

They said unto him, Be still
While winds of terror tore out shutters
Of his neighbour's home.

Beyond their walls to insulate
He felt his eyelids shrivel
In fires of rapine. The wrongs of day
And cries of night burnt red fissures
In chambers of his mind.

And so he set upon the quest
Seeking that whose plenitude
Would answer calls of hate and terror.

He looked with longing
To the lay of ocean pastures
Sought to harness their unbidden depths,

To measure the wind for symmetry
And on the wheel of earth to place
A compass for bewildered minds

He wondered in a treasure-house
Of inward prizes, strove to bring
Fleeting messages of time
To tall expressions, to granite arches
Spanned across landslides of the past

Even in the blind spoliation, amidst
Even the harrying of flames, he wished
To regulate the turn of hours

He lit the torch to a summons
Of the great procession – and, what of it?
What of it if thus he died
Burnt offering on the altar of fears?

FOR CHRISTOPHER OKIGBO

Perhaps 'tis kinder that vultures toil
To cleanse torch-bearers for the soil

Than eagles bare their living bone
Chained to an eternity of stone

Kinder that dying eyes should close
To truths of light on weed and rose

Than read in their own live entrails
Fulfilments of the web of nails

Kinder indeed full reckoning paid
A circle closed, a lowered shade

Leaving their world as blank a slate
As eyelids on the wall of Fate

Kinder that, lured by cleansing rites
He fell, burnt offering on the heights

His torch to waken mountain shrines
Fused to an alien tuber of mines

Yet kinder this, than a spirit seared
In violated visions and truths immured

Eternal provender for Time
Whose wings his boundless thoughts would climb.